Dear Tiff,

Thank you so much [...]
about your experienc[...]
you were the very firs[...] small business owner
I spoke with about the book and your
transparency was very encouraging to me
as I thought about reaching out to others.
I truly appreciate your friendship over
the years and wish you all the best with
your Real estate business

With Gratitude,

Bill

Bring Your Own Cyber

Bill Bonney

technology? Not without taking some precautions. The good news is you only need three or four tools to make travel safe.

To understand the strategy for defending ourselves when out and about, let's understand why it is dangerous out there. First, you have no idea what precautions providers have taken (or not taken) to protect the services they offer. Was the hotel WiFi configured properly (as we discussed in Chapter 3, Protecting Your Network)? Second, public access points, by definition, are open to the public. That means lots of potentially bad actors with unfettered access. They could be sitting right next to you, or they could have left something behind for anyone unlucky enough to encounter it. A common technique is to deploy a fake access point to intercept your traffic. If you're so inclined, search for "Wi-Fi pineapple" to read more.

OK, so primarily, we're interested in being safe on unsafe networks and avoiding the hidden (often baited – "free Wi-Fi") traps left behind.

We mentioned three or four tools to make travel safe. These include:

- A VPN – virtual private network for safe use of public access points.
- A USB "charge only" adapter – this device stops unwanted data transfers (e.g., passing a virus to your phone) from occurring over your charging cable when you plug into a public charging station.
- A portable battery pack – a better way to charge your phone on the go is a portable charger you charge up before you leave to give your phone a private boost.
- A WiFi device detector – this is an app you can download and install on your smartphone that allows you to scan any hotel room, Airbnb rental, or another public place for hidden WiFi cameras or other devices.

A VPN requires you to have an account with a VPN provider but is well worth the cost and trouble if you rely on access while outside the home or office. Using your cellular service instead of public WiFi is a helpful first step but does not entirely protect you as cell towers can be spoofed, meaning a thief can trick your phone into connecting to a fake tower and intercept your traffic.

In the last chapter, we listed some VPNs to consider, including NordVPN, CyberGhost, IPVanish, and ProtonVPN. As always, these are not endorsements, just a way to start your search. Make sure any provider you select is well rated by consumers and experts and provides coverage in your area and for the devices you will be using.

Any search of the Apple app store or for Android apps will show you many hidden camera detectors. Again, read the reviews of both consumers and experts before you download an app (especially for Android where the store is less curated) to make sure the app is legit. Look up the provider and make sure it is well-rated.

Take a similar approach to battery packs. I suggest getting two, one that is always charging and one you take with you. When you return home, swap them. If you can control the power source, you will not have to worry about plugging into a dirty power port. If you feel you must use a public power port, buy a few USB "charge only" adapters and make sure you always have one with you.

Creating and Managing Strong and Unique Passwords

In Chapter 1, we laid out seven steps for good cyber hygiene. Step 5 is to set strong, unique passwords, and change them regularly. But let's face it, passwords are a pain, and the average person today has more than 100 passwords to manage. We can't show you how to make the pain completely go away, but we can help you be more secure and spend less time and effort managing your passwords. Ironically, this section, while one of the most important, is going to be one of the shortest. We're not going to give you a long dissertation or fancy mnemonic technique to create an uncrackable password. That is so last decade.

The reality is that short passwords, and by that we mean anything less than 15 characters, are not secure. For years it was acceptable to say that the computer time required to crack a password of eight, then 10, then 13 characters was measured in the millions or billions of years. But when the prize is big enough, effort and money are deployed. Billions of passwords have been stolen, and techniques have been developed that create tables (called rainbow tables) that act like master keys for any password up to a certain length. It used to be that if you came up with one pretty complex password, you could use it everywhere and be secure. But as we explained in Chapter 2, the cyberthieves have a technique called credential stuffing and they use their trove of stolen passwords to try any password of yours they've ever stolen on every system they can think of that you might use.

With all these passwords out there on the black market and techniques to quickly break passwords up to and exceeding 13, 14, even 15 characters, how do you create and maintain more than 100 strong, unique passwords? Forget all those techniques you've learned about substituting numbers for letters and memorizing a nursery rhyme and using the first letter for every word to create passwords. The thieves know these techniques as well. Our recommendations for password management are as follows:

1. Use a password manager to create and manage your passwords. There are several different types of password managers, and some that even allow you to manage the passwords for your firm. You can use a cloud-based password manager or one that stores the passwords on your devices. We'll list several below, but again, these are not endorsements, just a way to start your own search.

2. Use the highest setting for each account. If the system you are using does not state it's maximum, chose one of at least 18 characters.

3. Don't reuse passwords. If you allow your password manager to choose your password, this won't be an issue, but don't cheat and reuse a strong password generated for one account on another.

4. Use unknowable information for your security questions. The best questions are ones you pick. Create an odd question and make up a bizarre answer and record it in your password manager. If you must use one of their preset questions, simply make up an answer – yes, lie. And then record that answer in your password manager.

A few additional recommendations:

- If you are just starting to use a password manager, focus first on your weak passwords (short passwords, those with simple words, common keyboard combinations) and then hit your sensitive accounts.

- How often you change your passwords depends on the type of account. For sensitive accounts, try to do it every 90 days. For others, change it if they disclose an incident, or you notice something suspicious.

- If your password manager has an automatic change option, use it.

- For consumer accounts you use infrequently, consider simply using their reset password feature when you need to log on.

- For added security, consider creating a single purpose email account you only use for password resets.

Start your search for password managers by looking up Keeper, LastPass, Dashlane, and 1Password, or use the rating service from CNET magazine (an excellent source of expert advice we rely on) and choose from their Top 10 list. Read the descriptions of the pros and cons and decide what is best for you.

In the next chapter, Web and Social Media Security, we'll talk about how to keep your online presence secure, but for now, here is a summary of the key steps we've covered to help you manage access and use strong passwords.

Basic Steps

- Assign every employee their own unique account
- Limit the number of people with privileged or administrator accounts to people with a need to know
- Choose a password manager for yourself and insist that all employees use one that suits them

Intermediate Steps

- Subscribe to a VPN service and use it whenever you are not in the home or office
- Disable all unused system accounts
- Use unique passwords for all accounts, no exceptions

Pro Steps

- Bring a battery pack with you and never use a public charging port
- Install a WiFi detector on your smartphone and scan hotel rooms, public spaces and Airbnb rooms for hidden devices

Section 2

Securing Your Brand

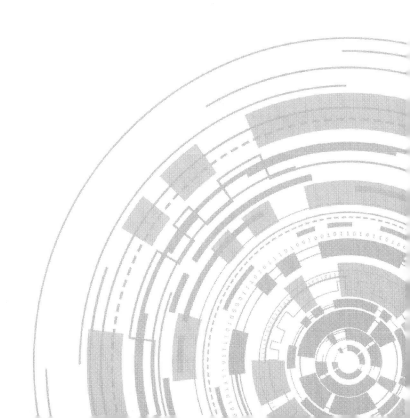

Introduction

Damage to your business can come in many forms. You can get robbed or fire can savage your shop, but perhaps the greatest damage is impact to your brand. Traditional insurance can reimburse you for theft and rebuild your burned-out shop. But recovering from brand damage is much more difficult.

Everything happens faster online. Going viral is great if mom's cookie recipe becomes an overnight international sensation. But the impact on your brand from a cyber incident can spread just as fast and have a devastating effect.

In Section 2, we're first going to talk about your online presence. Whether you have a company website or not, even if you think you have no online presence, you still have an online brand to manage, and security plays a major role in managing your online brand. Chapter 6 covers web and social media security.

After your online brand, we'll tackle data privacy in Chapter 7. Privacy is a hot topic, and I don't see that changing any time soon. People are still deciding what they want their public persona to mean to them. Whether that's about their latest post on social media, their latest online purchase, or their medical records, they want to know those records are safe and used the way they want them used. We have to know how to keep their data safe. It is their data.

In Chapter 8, we'll demystify cyber insurance. More small businesses are choosing to carry cyber insurance, and it's a decision that each small business owner needs to make based on their specific circumstances. As you'll see from the case studies presented in Chapter 7, not every firm needs cyber insurance. After reading Chapter 8, you can decide for yourself based on the descriptions of the types of coverage and the questions you'll need to answer to apply.

Finally, in Chapter 9, we'll summarize everything we've covered so you have a good action plan for turning these recommendations into the habits you will need to remain safe and secure online.

Chapter 6

Web and Social Media Security

When I started my first consulting business, in the mid 1980s, I placed an ad (written as an editorial, what is called an advertorial) in a local community paper and ran a small scrolling ad on community TV. I considered an eighth- or quarter-page ad in the yellow pages, but those were expensive, and I wanted to see if I could justify the ROI first. It's likely that a healthy percentage of small business owners reading this book have not advertised in their yellow pages or placed a classified ad in the local newspaper in years (if ever). These are still important advertising channels, but the landscape has changed drastically over the ensuing decades.

With the advent of online commerce, first the Internet and then social media, the calculus hasn't changed about where or how to engage with your customers or potential customers. You want to be where your customers and prospects are and engage them in a way that gets your message across. The big difference is that what once was mostly a one-way, often static message has become a two-way dynamic dialog. Instead of advertising *to* your customers you are now engaging *with* your customers. The combination of the geographic reach of the Internet and the amplifying effect of social media has, in many cases, allowed smaller companies to thrive like never before. The downside is that these digital media come with security concerns that need to be managed.

Broadly speaking, you need to be aware of and manage your presence across these categories of digital assets:

- **Company website** – for small businesses this is often a simple brochure site (describing products and services) or an eCommerce site (listing products for sale along with a shopping cart capability)
- **Social media sites** – such as Facebook, Twitter, LinkedIn, Instagram, and YouTube
- **Business listing or third-party review sites (TPRS)** – such as Yelp* For Business and Google My Business ™
- **E-commerce platforms** – such as Amazon, Etsy, and eBay
- **Payment services** – such as Clover, Venmo, PayPal, and Square

We're all likely aware of the more popular social media sites. Facebook, Twitter, Instagram, and YouTube are household names for every generation, even for those of us who don't use that particular service. Given that new sites seemingly pop up overnight and sometimes fall out of favor just as quickly, I am not going to try to list all the sites. In the pages that follow I will go through each of the five categories listed above and describe the main risks you need to be concerned with and prudent steps you should consider.

Company Web Site

Whether or not you have your own company website, or use a social media page as your main digital presence, should be driven by what is right for your business. Don't assume you must have "mybusiness.com" or "mybusiness.biz" when it might be cheaper and more effective to use Facebook or Twitter or Instagram, or even a Google My Business or Yelp* for Business page as your main online presence. If there is a compelling reason to have a company website, there are a few risks you need to guard against.

Regardless of whether you offer products for direct sale on your website, you should take two precautions with your web hosting service. First, make sure your website is registered privately. This is not the same thing as having an unlisted phone number. This keeps your personal information, such as your email address and phone number, separate from your website registration and helps protect you from lots of unwanted attention from scammers trying to sell services and other unwanted activities. For larger companies who have departments to handle all the various domains they control, public registry is a benefit and in some cases a requirement. But for small businesses, it's almost always best to register privately. If you feel you want to be public about your domain ownership, then consider getting a virtual phone number (e.g., Google Voice), an email address you don't use for regular activity, and a P.O. box so the solicitations don't disrupt your everyday life.

The second precaution is to opt for extra security, including the SSL certificate (also known as SSL security) and security monitoring from your web hosting company. Ever since internet commerce started taking off in the 1990s, having the lock icon displayed in the address field after navigating to an e-commerce site (making purchases online) essentially became required. This ensured that the transaction was encrypted between your device and the e-commerce site. How-to guides and news reports continually cautioned people not to shop unless they saw the lock. Starting in 2014, the Internet Architecture Board has called upon *all* web traffic to be encrypted, whether or not it supports banking or e-commerce. The point is to protect all online activity, including finance, e-commerce, social media, or purely informational downloads and non-sensitive conversations from eavesdropping and fraud. If you have a web site and do not opt for the SSL option, the site will either be marked with a broken lock (or a lock with a red line through it) or a label that says the site is not secure. This would likely scare many customers off.

Security protection and monitoring is also essential. What you want your hosting company to do for you is scan for vulnerabilities, block SPAM, and take other precautions so you don't get hassled and your site is not hijacked by thieves. Web listing services routinely monitor the overall health of the Internet and note if malware is detected on your site or if thieves start sending SPAM from your site. This will reflect badly on you and some services will warn people not to visit your site, while other services will actually prohibit their users from visiting your site. I suggest you pay for the extra security. It usually runs a few hundred dollars a year.

Now that you've chosen the right security options, the next security issue to think about is how you interact on the site. If you want to provide an option for customers or prospects to fill out an input form of any kind, or interact with you directly from your site, make sure your web designer turns on data validation and installs the right plugins (features that come as pre-packaged code for websites) to prevent fraudulent input and that your web hosting company is monitoring breach attempts on your site.

Social Media Sites

As I mentioned above, it is not at all necessary for most small businesses to have their own web site. And as I described in the preceding section, there are additional expenses and extra effort required to do it safely. Consider using one or more social media sites to create the online presence you need. The advantages are that the major social media company(s) you are likely to choose from are investing the money you would be spending on security (and much more) for you and have large staffs of highly trained individuals who are taking the necessary actions to operate safely and protect their platform. True, the larger target of the social media companies draws more attacks, but the impact of successful attacks is much worse for small shops maintaining their own site.

Whether you use a social media site as your main online presence or not, you will still probably need to engage with your customers and prospects using social media. Here is what you need to consider as you build your online presence.

1. Manage your password and access to your account.

We covered access in Chapter 5 so you will recognize the recommendations in this chapter. You'll want to make sure you have a strong password to your social media sites and that you turn on two-factor authentication if you can.

If you have a lot of volume on the site and have one or more members of your staff acting as you, it might be difficult to use two-factor authentication. If that's the case, make sure you coordinate changing your password with the people helping you, and consider more frequent password changes than you would otherwise. This is where using a password manager as recommended in Chapter 5 becomes very important. One where you can automatically share certain passwords with certain people would be a great way to manage access to your accounts.

Additionally, you'll want to set up notifications to the email and phone number that are on file and act quickly when you are notified of activity you didn't approve. It's also important for both you and your staff to be vigilant for any unexpected posts from your account.

2. Consistently monitor all the social media sites where you have an account.

It is tempting to ignore or abandon sites that don't show much activity for you personally or your business. But if you abandon the account it makes it a little easier for a thief to do an account takeover. Plus, you don't want to allow disparaging comments to go unchallenged. Be professional in your response, judgements are quick and harsh in the online world.

3. Apply the maximum privacy settings that don't interfere with your business.

Remember the adage that if you are not paying for the product, you are the product. Social media sites offer a lot of free services.

Facebook, Twitter, and Instagram even provide business pages for free. It is well known that to make that model work, they must sell something. Yes, they sell ads, but they also sell you. By that I mean they sell all the data you authorize them to sell. So, opt to turn the privacy setting on unless you really need the capability you are turning off.

Business Listings and Third-Party Review Sites (TPRS)

The main security issue with these sites is to claim your business.

Much like social media, you cannot completely control how your customers will find you, find out about you, or talk about you. It is important that you claim your business on all the major sites. On most sites there is a link or a button that asks, "is this you?" or allows you to click to claim this as your business. This is not only prudent marketing best practice, but by claiming your business you can avoid having bad actors disparage or exploit your good name. It is not uncommon for thieves to claim a company name with a good reputation and lure unsuspecting prospects to their scams. Claiming your company also allows you to provide consistent information across all platforms. And while this can become burdensome for businesses in certain industries, such as travel, for instance, where it seems like there are a million sites, you gain the security and you gain the marketing umph.

While not strictly a security issue, make sure you know how you are rated on each site and what those ratings mean. Just because the site provides a 5-point scale does not mean the average is 3. For some sites, anything less than 5 is judged negatively, and an average of around 4.7 starts to impact the types of clients who are sent your way.

One final point on this topic. At times you will receive a negative review and you may be tempted to pay for a service to scrub your site. Be very careful with this. These services are generally scams and the basic technique is to flood your company profile or products with positive reviews to push the negative review aside. This usually gets flagged as fraudulent and you'll end up making the matter much worse.

The best approach is to be proactive and responsive but not reactive. Being proactive means asking for positive reviews when things go well and customers are happy. This creates a bank of good will that can act as a buffer against negative reviews. Being responsive means addressing the negative reviews head on but professionally. Engage with the reviewer if you can, try to make things right, and when you do ask for an update. Look carefully at the review itself and if you think the review violates the TPRS's terms of service, file a complaint and the TPRS may remove it. Finally, don't be reactive, meaning don't attack the reviewer or threaten legal action against the reviewer or the TPRS. Keep it professional and you'll get better outcomes.

E-commerce Platforms and Payment Services

Treat e-commerce platforms and payment services as you would your bank. Turn on all security features, including two-factor authentication, extra control on money transfers, and appropriate notifications. You want to be alerted when money comes in (unless there is too much volume for you to appropriately monitor) and especially when money is transferred from your payment platform to your bank or when checks are issued. Follow up on any unauthorized activity immediately.

E-commerce sites also act as a TPRS and provide a way for customers to leave reviews and ratings. These reviews and ratings are often critical to the selling process. I recommend the same approach – be proactive and encourage your happy customers to leave reviews so that the inevitable mishaps and unsatisfied customers won't have a disproportionate impact on sales.

If you take payment cards through a point of sale (POS) terminal, whether it is a cash register or a smartphone, tablet, or PC running a payment app, make sure the service and your POS system is PCI compliant.

Where Do You Engage Digitally?

Web Hosting Services

WordPress, GoDaddy, HostGator, Bluehost

Social Sites

Facebook, Instagram, LinkedIn, Medium, Messenger, Pinterest, Reddit, Snapchat, Telegram, Tumblr, Twitter, Viber, WhatsApp, YouTube

Don't forget: Baidu, QQ, Qzone, Tieba, TikTok, WeChat

Review Sites

Amazon, Angies List, BBB, Facebook, Foursquare, Google My Business ™, Manta, Yellow Pages, Yelp

And for travel and reservations: Airbnb, Expedia, Kayak, OpenTable, Travelocity, TripAdvisor

Platforms

Airbnb, Amazon, Angies List, Doordash, eBay, Etsy, Grubhub, HomeAdvisor, Instacart, Lyft, OpenTable, Thumbtack, TaskRabbit, Uber, Vrbo, Wag

Payment Tools

Apple Pay, Google Wallet, PayPal, Square, Venmo

In the next chapter, Data Privacy, we'll do a deep dive on privacy regulations, thresholds for credit cards, CCPA, and GDPR, and how HIPAA applies to you, but for now, here is a summary of the key steps we've covered to help you securely manage your social media presence.

Basic Steps

- Carefully manage who has the ability to access your social media accounts and act on your behalf
- Treat all payment services as you treat your bank, enable extra security, including two-factor authentication, and follow up on alerts

Intermediate Steps

- Monitor all of the major social media sites for activity about you and engage with clients and prospects as needed
- Claim your company on all business listings and third-party review sites (TPRS) so you can control the messaging and stop cyber-squatters from exploiting your good name
- Use a password manager to control who has access to your social media accounts, change the password often, and monitor all alerts

Pro Steps

- If you have a company website, upgrade to a web hosting plan that includes SSL security and security monitoring
- Apply the maximum privacy settings on your social media accounts and don't share data about you that doesn't benefit you and your business
- Develop a proactive social media engagement plan that routinely asks (but doesn't nag) for positive reviews to manage your ratings and create a buffer against poor reviews

Chapter 7

Data Privacy

As much as we'd all like to think rules and regulations are for larger companies, or at least other companies, it's hard to completely avoid them and still be in business. As a small business owner, you're subject to quite a few, including tax withholding and workplace safety, to name just two. In addition, you could run into PCI (Payment Card Industry) depending on how you process credit cards for payment, or HIPAA (Health Information Portability and Accountability Act) if you are a health care provider. And finally, there are state, federal, and international data privacy and breach notification laws. These also include more recent (2018-2020) regulations known as CCPA (the California Consumer Privacy Act) and GDPR (the General Data Protection Regulation for the European Union). Just what we need, lots of 4- and 5-character acronyms!

Every State Has a Take

Besides the CCPA, which is intended to define California residents' rights over their data, every state in the U.S. (as of March 2018 – welcome to the party, Alabama and South Dakota) All states have mandatory breach notification requirements where the defined criteria are met (typically there are safe harbor provisions for encrypted data) and many states, similar to California, are establishing their own privacy regulations with expectations for 'reasonable' security. The CCPA and GDPR are different, they include far more extensive privacy rights for data subjects and consumers over how their data is used. That's an important difference as we'll see a little later. While small businesses are typically not banks, GLBA (the Gramm-Leach-Bliley Act) might still apply if you hold financial non-public information (NPI). Enforcement can reach all layers of government in the US, including all fifty states and the federal government, including even (and especially) the FTC enforcing Section 5 of the FCTA dealing with unfair and deceptive trade practices.

In this chapter, we're going to go over the basics, which includes what these rules and regulations mean and how small companies can comply without hiring teams of lawyers and consultants.

What is listed above includes handling credit cards (PCI), medical records (HIPAA), and personal information (data privacy and breach notification). Let's spell it out.

The oldest of these rules is Title II of the U.S. code that defines HIPAA, which dates back to 1996 and set standards for the electronic exchange of healthcare information, called electronic Protected Health Information (or ePHI). This was meant to introduce efficiencies in the healthcare ecosystem, along with the associated compliance requirements to safeguard the data being more efficiently exchanged.

Looking at the states, California introduced its breach notification law (SB 1386) in 2002, Nevada (N.R.S. § 603A) in 2005, Massachusetts (201 CMR 17) in 2009, and Texas (Texas Medical Records Privacy Act) in 2012. Each of these established key thresholds for compliance and were followed by a scramble over what they meant and how to comply. Then came waves of regulations from the other states that didn't want to feel left out. California, Nevada, Massachusetts, and Texas advanced key provisions that the other states then embraced.

The point of all of these privacy breach notification laws is to require companies to disclose when consumers' data has been inappropriately accessed. Through that potential public shaming and associated fines and potential additional regulatory oversight, companies are first nudged and then compelled to take more steps to protect the consumer information with which they have been entrusted. Most small businesses, excluding healthcare providers and professional services firms, probably won't run afoul of breach notification laws unless they store personal information about their customers. Doctors, lawyers, and accountants tend to store a lot of personal information, while hair stylists, lawn services, and electricians probably don't. So, don't panic, just stay informed.

Here is a case study of a small business and how they meet they cybersecurity and data privacy requirements.

CASE STUDY

Company Profile

Two-person law firm

Background and Cybersecurity/Data Privacy Issues

This law firm handles family law, wills, and estate planning. As such, they are entrusted with and must therefore protect highly sensitive and personal information that includes protected health information (PHI) and non-public personal (financial) information (NPI). They also take credit cards for payment. Document exchange is a very important service they offer their clients. They are subject to HIPAA, GLBA (banking), and PCI compliance, along with California breach notification laws, and if they ever take on a class action suit for California residents, the CCPA as well.

Solutions That Work

- Hired an IT support company to assist with installing software, performing backups, configuring secure file exchange, and making sure security features, including data encryption, were turned on and properly configured. Retained the IT firm for monthly support.

- Chose a payment platform that provides PCI compliance and was endorsed by a local bar association.

- Working with their insurance provider to add a cyber rider to cover data breaches, including PHI and NPI as well as customer profile information.

What They Would Do If an Incident Occurred

If a cyber incident occurred, they would call their IT support company and their insurance agent to figure out how to recover and what to do for clients and regulators.

I mentioned above that CCPA and GDPR are a little different than the other state and federal regulations. Although many think the CCPA is the California version of the GDPR, that's not the case. GDPR was enacted before CCPA, and the framers of CCPA certainly learned from the GDPR, but, being GDPR compliant does not mean you comply with CCPA.

What GDPR and CCPA have in common and how they differ from the myriad state and federal breach notification laws is that they both endow citizens (consumers) with rights over their data while the predecessor state regulations were conceived of as merely protections to prevent harm to citizens. These rights include the right to not have your data collected, the right to obtain a copy of the data a firm holds about you, and the right to have that data deleted by the firm.

The major differences between the GDPR and CCPA is that the CCPA uses an opt-out model (consumers can opt-out of data collection campaigns and the sale of their data) and has provisions for citizens to be compensated for their data, while GDPR has an opt-in model (consumers opt-in to having their data collected) and gives citizens the right to have erroneous data corrected. The CCPA also establishes the right that the California resident be informed regarding the nature of the information that is collected about them and the source of this information. The CCPA also establishes the notion of non-discrimination when the data subject or consumer exercises their privacy rights.

The Banks Got in the Act as Well

While all the states were sewing together this patchwork quilt of data privacy laws, in 2004 the payment card industry put the Payment Card Industry Data Security Standard (PCI-DSS) in place because payment card fraud had been increasing at an alarming rate. Sadly, we're not even close to out of the woods. Credit card fraud is still a multi-billion-dollar problem.

What Applies to You?

The first issue you need to worry about is whether you trigger the various thresholds for compliance. In the chart labeled figure 7.1, we've put together some general guidelines. This does not substitute for legal advice and you still should read the regulations for your locale. But this should be a good rule of thumb guide.

These compliance requirements have a lot in common. They all aim at protecting private consumer, patient, or citizen data, and they all come with associated reporting, fines, and various types of enforcement. From the perspective of data security, they have similar requirements for how to comply. Where they mostly differ is in the specifics about what happens when there is a breach.

These include the different thresholds for what constitutes a reportable event, how quickly the event must be reported, under what circumstances the individual consumers must be notified vs. the regulator, what the restitution will be to the consumer, and what fine or other sanction might be levied by regulators.

Privacy Trigger	If	Then	If	Then	If	Then
How do the regulations apply to your business?						
Credit Cards	0 annual credit card transactions	No PCI-DSS compliance requirements	1-20,000 annual credit card transactions #	PCI Level 4 compliance required	20,000 - 1,000,000 annual credit card transactions	PCI level 3 compliance required
Medical Records	• Do not provide healthcare services • Do not provide services that access PHI for a covered entity	No HIPAA compliance requirements	Healthcare provider (Covered Entity)	HIPAA compliance required	Provide services to healthcare provider (Business Associate)	HIPAA compliance required
Personal Information about Consumers	Collect data on resident of any state	Potentially subject to the data privacy laws of the state	Consult a reference such as this one: https://www.mintz.com/sites/default/files/media/documents/2019-03-27/APRIL19_-_State_Data_Breach_Matrix.pdf that lists thresholds and requirements for every state.			
Personal Information about Californians*	Processes personal information of 50,000 or more consumers, households, or devices	CCPA compliance not required	>50,000 annual credit card transactions or more than $25M in annual revenue	CCPA compliance required	50% or more of business activity involves personal data	CCPA compliance required
Personal Information about EU Citizens**	• No presence in an EU country • < 250 employees	No GDPR compliance requirements	A presence in an EU country	GDPR compliance requirement	• Process personal data of EU residents • Have >250 employees	GDPR compliance requirement

Figure 7.1

* The CCPA does not apply to information that is subject to other federal regulations, including HIPAA, GLBA, the Fair Credit Reporting Act (FCRA), or the Drivers' Privacy Protection Act (DPPA), unless you collect and process other personal information about consumers. But it does apply to payment card information. A doctor's office, for instance, does not have to apply CCPA rules to their PHI, but does have to apply them to their payment card information.

** The GDPR can apply even if no financial transaction occurs. Let's say you are a U.S. company selling or marketing products over the Web, or just interacting with people (say, via a survey) – you may be subject to the GDPR. General global marketing does not usually apply. If you buy search words and an EU resident happens upon your web page, the GDPR likely would not apply for that alone. But if you target EU residents – and provide services directed to them (shipping, accepting their currency, providing translation to make transactions easier) – the GDPR will apply to you. If you are engaged in monitoring the behavior of EU residents (e.g., tracking and collecting information about EU users to predict their online behavior), the GDPR likely will apply.

Don't let the 20,000 (PCI) and 50,000 (CCPA) cutoffs fool you. 20,000 credit card transactions are reached with just 55 transactions a day and the 50,000 data records includes consumers, households *and devices.*

Here is a case study of another small business, this time an electrolysis service and bridal store and how they meet their requirements.

CASE STUDY

Company Profile

Electrolysis practice and bridal store

Background and Cybersecurity/Data Privacy Issues

This is both a personal services (electrolysis) business and a retail (bridal store) business. As such, the proprietor must comply with a larger superset of regulations. Because the electrolysis business is not considered a health care provider, it does not fall under HIPAA. Both businesses take credit cards and debit cards, and they operate in the state of California, so they do potentially fall under CCPA. They use both payment apps on mobile devices for the electrolysis services and a Point of Sale (POS) terminal in the bridal shop. While this book is being written, combating the COVID-19 pandemic is causing many businesses to implement various personal safety measures.

Solutions That Work

- Routinely follows the CA State Board of Barbering and Cosmetology for guidance about safely providing services to consumers.

- Works with their bank and their payment system vendor to understand what they should do to safeguard payment card data, including any updates to procedures.

- When choosing their bank and their payment system, they specifically limited their selection to those that provided solutions that were PCI compliant.

- Chose not to carry cyber insurance as they do not retain customer records with sensitive data, and they do not retain payment card information in their office.

What They Would Do If an Incident Occurred

If a cyber incident occurred, they would call their local law enforcement, their bank, and their payment system vendor.

How to Comply

The second issue you need to worry about is how to comply. The chart in Figure 7.2 shows a checklist that you should apply to your operations.

Don't be intimidated by these requirements. A self-assessment questionnaire (SAQ) simply requires you to review the status of your payment card protections and self-report what controls are in place and controls you may be working to implement. The expectation is that you can answer yes to each question. If the question addresses an important area, the PCI-DSS standards council may require you to explain your remediation plans for any "no" answers. There are eight different questionnaires and you'll use the one that describes how you handle credit cards. Quarterly scans and validated submissions are typically done for you by your merchant service unless you are large enough to manage your own website with a payment page you present and maintain. I highly recommend that you avoid this and outsource any web-based payment processing to a service provider approved by the PCI standards council.

Compliance Level	Requirements to Comply
Level 3 PCI	Complete Annual Self-Assessment Questionnaire
	Conduct Quarterly Scans
	Provide Validated Submission
Level 4 PCI	Complete Annual Self-Assessment Questionnaire
	Conduct Quarterly Scans
HIPAA	Adhere to the HIPAA Privacy and Security Rules
	Execute Business Associate Agreements with any third party with whom the organization shares PHI
CCPA	Implement the Micro-Business Compliance Checklist
GPDR	Implement the Micro-Business Compliance Checklist

Figure 7.2

As either a healthcare "covered entity" or a "business associate" you need to have a Business Associate Agreement (BAA) in place with any entity that you give access to the PHI you control. You also need to adhere to the HIPAA Privacy Rule, HIPAA Security Rule, and HIPAA Breach Notification Rule. These are listed in Appendix B.

HIPAA Security Rule

- Ensure the confidentiality, integrity, and availability of all ePHI you create, receive, maintain, or transmit
- Identify and protect against reasonably anticipated threats to the security or integrity of the ePHI
- Protect against reasonably anticipated, impermissible uses or disclosures
- Ensure compliance by your workforce

Here is a final case study that profiles a dental office and shows how they comply with their requirements.

What follows the case study are two pages that summarize the security controls and privacy checklist that apply to micro businesses. As with all cybersecurity recommendations, these are not meant to guarantee compliance or security, but implementing these controls and applying this checklist should give you reasonable assurance that you are taking due care with your business and with your customers' data.

CASE STUDY

Company Profile

Sole practitioner dental office with one dentist, one assistant, one hygienist, and one office manager

Background and Cybersecurity/Data Privacy Issues

This is a dental practice in the state of California that also sees patients from the European Union (EU). They are therefore entrusted with patient records which contain protected health information, or PHI. Since they take payment cards, including credit cards, debit cards, FSA cards, and HSA cards, they are concerned about PCI requirements. Because they operate in California and have patients that are citizens of the EU, they are concerned about the CCPA and GDPR, in addition to the California breach notification rules.

Solutions That Work

- Hired an IT support company to assist with installing software, performing backups, and making sure security features, including data encryption, were turned on and properly configured.

- Signed up for newsletters with the DEA (Drug Enforcement Agency) and DOJ (Department of Justice) to stay abreast of issues for prescribing controlled substances.

- Periodically review information put out by the California Dental Association and the American Dental Association; routinely talk shop with colleagues and scan the local newspaper for information about laws and regulations passed.

- Worked with their bank and their accounting software vendor to understand what they should do to safeguard payment card data. Implemented extra security options to protect their bank accounts.

- Worked with their insurance agent to include a cyber rider to cover a data breach of the PHI.

What They Would Do If an Incident Occurred

If a cyber incident occurred, they would call their IT support company and their insurance agent to figure out how to recover and what to do for patients and regulators.

Micro-Business Control Set

- Put important papers in locked drawers

- Secure your bank accounts by limiting or removing wire transfer capabilities

- Make sure all money movement requires a second verification step

- Implement a cybersecurity training program for all employees

- Change default passwords

- Install and use a firewall and anti-malware software

- Configure your routers and WiFi routers with advanced settings to restrict use outside your network

- Apply updates for perimeter and network devices as soon as they are available

- Implement a 3-2-1 backup strategy using a backup solution that automates daily, weekly and monthly backup processes

- Assign every employee their own unique account

- Limit the number of people with privileged or administrator accounts to people with a need to know

- Disable all unused system accounts

- Use unique passwords for all accounts, no exceptions, including social media and all online services

- Use restrictive privacy settings for all online services

- Turn on broad notifications for all financial and customer engagement activity

Micro-Business Compliance Checklist

1. Document the personal data that you hold, where it came from, and who you share it with.

2. Review how you seek, record, and manage consent, and whether you need to make any changes.

3. Consider how you will verify individuals' ages and how to obtain parental or guardian consent when needed for any data processing activity.

4. Create and document a procedure to provide an individual for whom you hold personal data a complete data set in a commonly readable format such as MS Word document, Google Doc, Excel spreadsheet, CSV file, or PDF file within 30 days of a request.

5. Create and document a procedure to delete all data you hold (except that which you are legally required to keep, such as PHI and tax related data) on any individual within 30 days, should a request be made.

6. Verify you have procedures in place to detect, report, and investigate a personal data breach.

7. Implement the micro-business control set defined above.

8. Review your current privacy disclosures and make any necessary changes.

9. Train your employees to protect personal information, to observe and report inappropriate access to personal information, and to understand their obligations under the regulations.

10. Create a list of parties you will notify in the case of a breach, whether you discover it, or it is reported to you by a service provider. Include at a minimum your insurance agent, your lawyer, law enforcement (working with your lawyer), your bank (or the provider of your merchant services) and the appropriate state authorities.

Specific to the CCPA
1. Create a clear and conspicuous homepage privacy link.

Specific to the GDPR
1. Identify the lawful basis for your processing activity and document it.

Privacy Disclosures

Pay close attention to the requirements for privacy disclosures for both CCPA and GDPR. They are specific.

The CCPA gives consumers the right to know exactly what personal information is being collected about them and the sources of this information. In order to comply with that, businesses must provide a disclosure before they collect the information. The disclosure must inform consumers as to the categories of personal information being collected and the purposes for which the personal information will be used. You must also disclose where that personal information is gathered from, the categories of third parties with whom it is shared, and any specific pieces of personal information collected.

The GDPR requires that you disclose to your users their eight rights under the GDPR, which are:

- The right to be informed.
- The right of access.
- The right to rectification.
- The right to erasure.
- The right to restrict processing.
- The right to data portability.
- The right to object.

When creating your notification checklist, you should include the reporting process for each state that extends protections for its residents to include your firm.

If you do business in more than one state or you have customers from other states, we strongly recommend that you work with a privacy law firm that is versed in privacy laws for those states. This firm can help you refine your checklist and meet your initial reporting deadlines as well as advise on which authorities to notify and when.

Resources

- The official **PCI** standards council site
  https://www.pcisecuritystandards.org/
- The official Department of Health and Human Services
  (HHS) site:
  https://www.hhs.gov/**hipaa**/for-professionals/security/laws-
  regulations/index.html
- The official **CCPA** site:
  https://oag.ca.gov/privacy/ccpa
- The official **GDPR** site:
  https://eur-lex.europa.eu/eli/reg/2016/679/oj
  Also see Wikipedia entry for help:
  https://en.wikipedia.org/wiki/General_Data_Protection_Re
  gulation
- A list of **state privacy legislation** (as of the printing of this
  book):
  https://en.wikipedia.org/wiki/State_privacy_laws_of_the_U
  nited_States
- **Web content accessibility guidelines**
  (WCAG)https://www.w3.org/WAI/standards-
  guidelines/wcag/

What this means is that you need to take the precautions your bank and insurance company recommend; implement the controls we've suggested in Chapters 1 though 6, and make sure your employees understand their responsibilities and act accordingly.

In the next chapter, Cyber Insurance, I'll provide a primer on cyber insurance, including what it covers and what it doesn't, when you should get it, and what you need to do to qualify, but for now, here is a summary of the key steps we've covered to help you guard your payment card data, safeguard protected health information, and comply with state privacy and breach notification laws.

Basic Steps

- Review figure 7.1 and determine how HIPAA, PCI, CCPA, and the GDPR apply to you.
- Make a list of all the states where you do business, or where your customers reside.
- Update your privacy notifications and disclosures to meet minimum disclosure requirements.

Intermediate Steps

- Review figure 7.2 and determine the actions you need to take to comply with privacy regulations.
- Make a list of all the personal information you collect on your customers, where you get it, how you use it, and who you share it with.
- Meet with a privacy lawyer and map out a notification checklist in the event of a breach of personal data you maintain.

Pro Steps

- Prepare for the eventual nation-wide rollout of legislation similar to the CCPA by implementing the micro-business compliance checklist.

Chapter 8

Cyber Insurance

Cyber insurance is one of the fastest growing segments of insurance for small businesses. The reasons won't surprise you. The largest driver is that more businesses are demanding cyber insurance as a requirement for doing business with suppliers and partners. Another driver is the increasing incidence of cybercrime against small businesses.

When I ran my first small business, I was required to have a general liability policy and when I started getting larger clients, I was forced to add errors and omissions coverage. I sure didn't get those policies because I wanted to. Who needs that expense? At the point that I was no longer offering services or servicing the customers who required the policy, I was left with the decision of whether to keep the coverage.

Insurance is a risk management tool, period. It is not a moral decision; we're not good or bad if we do or don't carry insurance. Whether or not you get cyber insurance (or any insurance for that matter) for your company should be a decision you come to after weighing the risks of adverse events (for example, the likelihood and impact of an inappropriate disclosure or losing a contract) against the cost of the premiums for the coverage obtained.

What Cyber Insurance Covers

Generally speaking, cyber insurance protects the company from losses incurred due to cyber incidents. Cyber insurance covers two distinct categories of expenses: first-party expenses (the organization's specific expenses) and third-party claims (the exposure to claims against the organization given a breach or other such incident).

First-party expense coverage is designed to cover those expenses that are tied directly to the organization, including cyber extortion coverage, business interruption coverage, and other business-related expenses associated with the breach. The latter includes items such as the costs of digital forensics (typically an expensive service) and the hard costs associated with breach response (for instance customer notifications and credit monitoring services).

Third-party expense coverage addresses penalties and regulatory actions related to privacy and security violations resulting from the inadequacy of privacy and security protections within the organization. Third-party coverage may also include content-related issues, including copyright infringements, libel, and slander. Policies generally have coverage limits, with sub-limits for specific first-party and third-party damage.

The types of cyber incidents fall into three categories:

Category one – Probably the most easily understood is the loss due to the inappropriate disclosure of private or protected information. This is typically called a data breach, and while that sounds like a bad actor of some kind is involved, this category also covers unintentional breaches, such as inadvertently exposing protected health information to an unauthorized employee or sending sensitive information to the wrong client or patient. Coverage in these cases includes all or part of the costs to notify the people who are the subjects of the breach, state or other regulatory fines, the cost of breach remediation, including fixing systems and providing identity monitoring, and in some cases, losses due to systems being offline while being remediated, effectively business interruption coverage.

Category two – Probably the most common for micro-businesses, this category includes business email compromise (BEC), as well as malware attacks (often but not always delivered via email) such as ransomware and crypto mining. Some insurance carriers call this entire category BEC, although cybersecurity professionals prefer to draw a distinction between BEC and phishing attacks. Coverage in this case might include the cost of scrubbing malware from your systems, recovering money lost, possibly even paying the ransom. The latter is a decision your insurance carrier would make with you depending on the cost of recovering versus the likelihood the cyber thieves would actually be willing and able to give you the unlock key. Many insurance companies are now brokering the payments and serving as an intermediary negotiating the ransom. It is a good idea to ask your agent about whether this service is included.

Category three – This includes protection against fines and judgements because content that you are responsible for, such as information or dialog posted on a company website or attributed to you on some system accessible on the internet becomes a matter of dispute. This would include information that is controversial in some way, such as offensive content or content that is claimed as the intellectual property of another party. Depending on your policy, this might also include protection against advertising and other statements made in the public domain for the purpose of promoting your business that might infringe on the rights of others. Coverage in this case might include lawyer's fees and judgements awarded in compensation to the aggrieved party.

While these are the general categories of risk that a small business cyber policy might cover, they are also the categories of risk that drive the cost of the policy. So, for instance, if a customer or third-party requires you to have a cyber insurance policy and your insurance carrier determines your risk in those three categories is non-existent, they will likely charge a lot less for the policy. Conversely, the more risk in each of these categories, the higher your premiums.

Determining Risk

To determine the risk exposure a small business has, the insurer will perform a risk assessment. This is usually done (at least initially) with an intake form that asks questions about the company's business activities and cyber hygiene practices. In some cases, the carrier may want to visit you to make a more thorough assessment of your risk of loss.

First up is usually general information about the company. The carrier would want to know the name and address of the business and the nature of the products and services provided. Certain industries are subject to more cyber activity than others. Additional demographic information is requested, such as number of employees, revenue, and gross profit. This is common to the general liability questionnaire if you've considered such coverage.

In addition to the general information, there are usually questions to help identify sources of risk. You'll likely be asked if you collect credit card information, personal information, or protected health information about customers or patients.

You'll also be asked about certain measures you take to protect your systems, such as backups, encryption, and endpoint protection. Additionally, the carrier will want to know how you protect your business legally, by asking, for instance, if all customers sign a contract (along with certain terms of the contract), and if you conduct background checks on prospective employees.

Every carrier has some list of procedures they require you to have in place before they will underwrite a policy for you. Common across most carriers are backups and endpoint protection. Most would add encryption of sensitive data if you collect and store credit card data or protected health information.

The last category of information the carrier would collect is your loss history. This again is common to your general liability policy. They will want to know if you have had a payout for a cyber incident within the last three years. And, of course, they all ask if you are aware of any issue that would cause a payout. They want to know if you are trying to close the proverbial barn door after the horses have left.

Another key element you need to be aware of are the exclusions in your policy. Some policies may exclude coverage for losses arising from shortcomings in your security program, usually if you were aware of these shortcomings before purchasing the policy, or you failed to take reasonable care. Make sure you know what is required to document that you are taking prudent action. Record the hygiene activities you have underway so you can show you were taking reasonable care. Most policies will also have exclusions for acts of terrorism or war. It's tempting to think this will not apply to you as you are not likely to be the victim of a nation state or a terrorist organization, but collateral damage from these events can impact you if you also rely on the systems or infrastructure that is damaged. So just be aware of this before you execute your policy.

Whether or not you can obtain the coverage you want will ultimately depend on the risk you present to the carrier. This will be determined by assessing the business you are in and the way you conduct your business. If you deal with payment card information or retain protected health information, for example, and do not take adequate steps to secure this information, you will likely be denied coverage until you are able to correct the deficiencies. As you've probably already figured out, implementing the micro-business control set, and applying the micro-business compliance checklist defined in Chapter 7 are the activities I would recommend you take to make qualifying for cyber liability insurance more likely. Keep records of your compliance activities so you can demonstrate your due care to the carrier.

Finally, keep in mind that different insurance carriers have different risk tolerance and differing levels of experience underwriting cyber insurance. Shop around. Interview the broker as they are interviewing you. Make sure that the broker is an expert in cyber insurance. These are still relatively new policies relative to insurance in general. Do your homework.

In the final chapter, Be Ready, we're going to summarize what we've covered in this book and recommend ways of readying yourself for a future event, but for now, here is a summary of the key steps we've covered to help you be a smart cyber insurance consumer and take the actions to keep losses and premiums at a minimum.

Basic Steps

- Determine whether you need cyber insurance (e.g., due to contractual needs or driven by your high-risk activities)
- If cyber insurance is a contractual requirement, verify your minimum coverages

Intermediate Steps

- Implement the micro-business control set
- Comparison shop with two or more carriers
- Interview the insurance agent as they evaluate you

Pro Steps

- Apply the micro-business compliance checklist
- Review checklist and control set records annually with your carrier and reevaluate premiums based on loss history and the safeguards you have in place

Chapter 9

Be Ready

We've covered a lot of ground in Chapters 1 through 8. Everything from locking the door to securing your presence on social media. This last chapter is pretty short. There are a few steps I recommend you repeat periodically so that you become and remain ready to deal with any cyber incident that comes your way. You'll recognize a lot of this advice; it mostly comes from the Pro Steps I've outlined throughout the book. You'll also see the pattern – routine! Develop routines around cyber safety. Just as personal hygiene depends on routine, so too does cyber hygiene.

- Routinely check the office or the store and make sure you have not become lax in locking things up. When devices aren't in use, when you're done with your paperwork, when no one is in the shop – lock it up.
- Check your email and your smartphone for notifications from your bank. Make sure that you are following up on any suspicious activity.
- Review one of the recommended publications from Chapter 2 each week. Stay up on the developments in the cybercrime world.
- Hold monthly or quarterly lunches with your employees and use the opportunity to learn what they are experiencing. Have they seen anything happen that you need to be aware of? Are they remaining diligent? The number one attack vector for small businesses (all businesses really) is email. No clicking on unexpected attachments.

- Routinely test your backups. Nothing is more frustrating than dead batteries in the flashlight when the power goes out and nothing is more destructive to your business than not having a good backup when something happens to your data.

- Don't let your guard down when you are traveling. Bring your own battery backup so that you are never plugging your device into a public charging station. Make sure you always sweep your hotel room, coffee shop, and Airbnb for hidden devices.

- Keep up on what your customers, prospects, and competitors are saying on social media and stay engaged. The old adage that the best defense is a good offense is never more apt than on social media.

- Routinely check the privacy settings for social media. The social media sites are selling data, data about you. They are constantly adding more engagement features and each feature comes with its own privacy settings. Minimize data leakage by checking the settings periodically.

- Stay aware of the advances in privacy legislation. Privacy is at the forefront of consumer protection now that our lives are so intertwined with technology. The news sources I listed in Chapter 2 will be covering developments and you should use those publications to stay informed and be proactive, so the privacy expectations of your customers don't pass you by.

- On an annual basis, review your notification checklist with your privacy lawyer and your insurance broker.

- In case of a cybersecurity incident, keep the list of "in the event of emergency" contacts up to date and include law enforcement on that list. Go to "ready.gov/cybersecurity" which is the site maintained by the department of homeland security. Steps to take after a breach can be found in Appendix A.

For those of you who are experiencing significant growth, this book might serve as a primer, but you may find yourself needing more concrete steps you can take to take your program to the next level. In that case, I highly recommend another book in the CISO Desk Reference catalog geared toward slightly larger companies with a need for a more mature program. Alan Watkins' book *Creating a Small Business Cybersecurity Program* takes you step-by-step through the process of creating a formal, structured program that will help you to that next level.

OK, there you have it. You are now ready to bring your own cyber and keep your business secure.

Conclusion

I dedicated this book to all the entrepreneurs who have entered the arena with a dream of greatness and a will to make it happen. As the owner of a micro-business, you know what it means to own every problem. I hope this book will help you rest a little easier when it comes to securing your business in the digital marketplace.

CISO DRG was founded to bring real-world advice from practitioners to help us all secure our digital future. This book, and its two companions: *The Essential Guide to Cybersecurity for SMBs*, by Gary Hayslip, and *Creating a Small Business Cybersecurity Program*, by Alan Watkins, complete the CISO Desk Reference Guide Small Business Series. We hope this catalog we are building makes a difference.

Appendix A – Ready.Gov Cybersecurity Page

https://www.ready.gov/cybersecurity

Excerpt taken from this site and then modified with additional recommendatios.

After a Cyberattack

- Contact your insurance agent if you have a cybersecurity insurance policy or rider.
- File a report with the Office of the Inspector General (OIG) if you think someone is illegally using your Social Security number. (https://www.idtheft.gov/)
- File a complaint with the FBI Internet Crime Complaint Center (IC3). They will review the complaint and refer it to the appropriate agency. (https://www.ic3.gov/)
- File a report with the local police so there is an official record of the incident.
- Report identity theft to the Federal Trade Commission. (http://www.ftc.gov/)
- Contact additional agencies depending on what information was stolen. Examples include contacting the Social Security Administration (800-269- 0271) if your social security number was compromised, or the Department of Motor Vehicles if your driver's license or car registration has been stolen. (http://oig.ssa.gov/report)
- Report online crime or fraud to your local United States Secret Service (USSS) Electronic Crimes Task Force (http://www.secretservice.gov/investigation/#field) or the Internet Crime Complaint Center.

- For further information on preventing and identifying threats, visit US-CERT's Alerts and Tips page. (http://www.us-cert.gov/alerts-and-tips/)

HIPAA Privacy Rule

The HIPAA Privacy Rule establishes standards to protect PHI held by these entities and their business associates:

- Health plans
- Health care clearinghouses
- Health care providers that conduct certain health care transactions electronically

The Privacy Rule gives individuals important rights with respect to their protected PHI, including rights to examine and obtain a copy of their health records in the form and manner they request, and to ask for corrections to their information. Also, the Privacy Rule permits the use and disclosure of health information needed for patient care and other important purposes.

PHI

The Privacy Rule protects PHI held or transmitted by a covered entity or its business associate, in any form, whether electronic, paper, or verbal. PHI includes information that relates to all of the following:

- The individual's past, present, or future physical or mental health or condition
- The provision of health care to the individual
- The past, present, or future payment for the provision of health care to the individual

PHI includes many common identifiers, such as name, address, birth date, and Social Security number.

Visit the Health and Human Services (HHS) HIPAA Guidance webpage for guidance on:

- De-identifying PHI to meet HIPAA Privacy Rule requirements
- Individuals' right to access health information
- Permitted uses and disclosures of PHI

HIPAA Security Rule

The HIPAA Security Rule specifies safeguards that covered entities and their business associates must implement to protect ePHI confidentiality, integrity, and availability.

Covered entities and business associates must develop and implement reasonable and appropriate security measures through policies and procedures to protect the security of ePHI they create, receive, maintain, or transmit. Each entity must analyze the risks to ePHI in its environment and create solutions appropriate for its own situation. What is reasonable and appropriate depends on the nature of the entity's business as well as its size, complexity, and resources. Specifically, covered entities must:

- Ensure the confidentiality, integrity, and availability of all ePHI they create, receive, maintain, or transmit
- Identify and protect against reasonably anticipated threats to the security or integrity of the ePHI
- Protect against reasonably anticipated, impermissible uses or disclosures
- Ensure compliance by their workforce

When developing and implementing Security Rule compliant safeguards, covered entities and their business associates may consider all of the following:

- Size, complexity, and capabilities
- Technical, hardware, and software infrastructure
- The costs of security measures
- The likelihood and possible impact of risks to ePHI

Covered entities must review and modify security measures to continue protecting ePHI in a changing environment.

- Visit the HHS HIPAA Guidance webpage for guidance on:
- Administrative, physical, and technical safeguards
- Cybersecurity
- Remote and mobile use of ePHI

HIPAA Breach Notification Rule

The HIPAA Breach Notification Rule requires covered entities to notify affected individuals; HHS; and, in some cases, the media of a breach of unsecured PHI. Generally, a breach is an impermissible use or disclosure under the Privacy Rule that compromises the security or privacy of PHI. The impermissible use or disclosure of PHI is presumed to be a breach unless you demonstrate there is a low probability the PHI has been compromised based on a risk assessment of at least the following factors:

- The nature and extent of the PHI involved, including the types of identifiers and the likelihood of re-identification
- The unauthorized person who used the PHI or to whom the disclosure was made
- Whether the PHI was actually acquired or viewed
- The extent to which the risk to the PHI has been mitigated.

Most notifications must be provided without unreasonable delay and no later than 60 days following the breach discovery. Notifications of smaller breaches affecting fewer than 500 individuals may be submitted to HHS annually. The Breach Notification Rule also requires business associates of covered entities to notify the covered entity of breaches at or by the business associate.

Visit the HHS HIPAA Breach Notification Rule webpage for guidance on:

- Administrative requirements and burden of proof
- How to make unsecured PHI unusable, unreadable, or indecipherable to unauthorized individuals
- Reporting requirements

Key Provisions in a Nutshell

State	Key Provision	Details
California	Breach notification	When published in 2002, SB 1386 provided the first set of state breach notification rules.
		https://en.wikipedia.org/wiki/California_S.B._1386
Massachusetts	Preventive controls requirements	201 CMR 17 raised the compliance bar in 2009 by establishing minimum standards that companies were required to take to try to prevent potential breaches.
		https://en.wikipedia.org/wiki/201_CMR_17.00 https://www.mass.gov/files/documents/2017/11/21/compliance-checklist.pdf
Nevada	More breach notification requirements	Published in 2005, these breach notification rules expanded on the California requirements, notably by requiring encryption for sensitive information.
		https://en.wikipedia.org/wiki/State_privacy_laws_of_the_United_States#Nevada
Texas	Medical records privacy	Texas set broader requirements so that more companies fell under the rules for notification about medical records leaks in 2012 when it passed the Texas Medical Records Privacy Act.
		https://texaslawhelp.org/article/state-and-federal-health-privacy-laws

Figure B.1

PCI Requirements for Level 2 and Level 1 Merchants

Goals	PCI DSS Requirements
Build and Maintain a Secure Network and Systems	1. Install and maintain a firewall configuration to protect cardholder data 2. Do not use vendor-supplied defaults for system passwords and other security parameters
Protect Cardholder Data	3. Protect cardholder data 4. Encrypt transmission of cardholder data across open, public networks
Maintain a Vulnerability Management Program	5. Protect all systems against malware and regularly update anti-virus software or programs 6. Develop and maintain secure systems and applications
Implement Strong Access Control Measures	7. Restrict access to cardholder data by business need to know 8. Identify and authenticate access to system components 9. Restrict physical access to cardholder data
Regularly Monitor and Test Networks	10. Track and monitor all access to network resources and cardholder data 11. Regularly test security systems and processes
Maintain an Information Security Policy	12. Maintain a policy that addresses information security for all personnel

Figure B.2

Bill Bonney is a security evangelist, author, and consultant. As co-author of the Cybersecurity Canon Hall of Fame books Volume 1 and 2 of the CISO Desk Reference Guide, Bill and co-authors Matt Stamper and Gary Hayslip are dedicated to providing the practical advice we  need to combat the ongoing scourge of cybercrime. Prior to co-founding CISO DRG Publishing, Bill was Vice President of Product Marketing and Chief Strategist at UBIQ (formerly FHOOSH), a maker of high-speed encryption software, Vice President of Product Marketing and Principal Consulting Analyst at TechVision Research, and Director of Information Security and Compliance at Intuit, maker of personal and small business financial products.

Bill holds multiple patents in data protection, access, and classification, and was an early member of the Board of Advisors for CyberTECH, a San Diego incubator. He was a founding member of the board of directors for the San Diego CISO Round Table, a professional group focused on building relationships and fostering collaboration in information security management. Bill is a highly regarded speaker and panelist addressing technology and security concerns. He holds a Bachelor of Science degree in Computer Science and Applied Mathematics from Albany University.

LinkedIn Profile: https://www.linkedin.com/in/billbonney

Made in the USA
Middletown, DE
11 October 2020